400 degrees
HOT CHICKEN
615-***-4467

N°. 5382

serve

12 flaky
2 cups ho
1/2 cup ea
1/4 cup fr

For each ind
Add another r
each of the ber

ALL ACCESS

LORRIE
MORGAN

BAGGAGE (STRAP) TAG

TO
PAR
PARIS, France

FLIGHT No.
153
TOTAL WEIGHT
44 KGs
TOTAL NUMBER OF
CHECKED PIECES
3

PSGR'S NAME
Thompson

BookBaby
877-961-6878
7905 N. Crescent Blvd.
Pennsauken, NJ 08110
www.bookbaby.com

Written by Lorrie Morgan
Design by Karen Cronin / Cronin Creative

Orders by U.S. trade bookstores and wholesalers. Please contact BookBaby
tel 877-961-6878 or visit www.bookbaby.com

First Edition July 2019

Made in the U.S.A.

TO EAT OR NOT TO EAT

That is The Question

WRITINGS AND RECIPES
FROM HOME & ON THE ROAD

LORRIE MORGAN

"IN EVERY COUNTRY KITCHEN IN
THE SOUTH, THESE ARE STAPLES"

Lorrie's Travels

"I'VE TRAVELED ALL AROUND THE WORLD
NOT ONLY TO SING MY MUSIC BUT IN SEARCH OF
SOME OF THE WORLD'S GREATEST FOODS... SOMETIMES."

Growing up in a family that centered itself and special occasions around wonderful dishes and smells from the kitchen, food has always been a center staple in my life.

"Come on in let me fix ya some biscuits ~~and eggs~~ with Sorgrum and coffee," to "Oh we have plenty fried chicken and dumplings left?!!"

My father's mother Ethel Morgan taught my mother Anna

how to cook and ever since I
can remember my mom spent
most of her time cooking up
my dad's favorite recipes
from either his childhood
or recipes he would
bring home from some
exotic place he had been on
the road.

My sisters Candy, Beth, Liana
and my brother Marty all learned
to cook and experiment in the
kitchen along side of my mom
Anna and my dad George.

My father would take us to
a ~~AAAAA~~ Restaurant one night
to teach us about table
manners and different types
of food and the next ~~night~~

week we would eat Chile in our car at the local Krystal. Consequently we grew up loving all different types of food from Oyster Rockerfeller to Rumaki to TennTuchy County Klam", one of my dad's favorites". My dad always said "Don't say you don't like something if you have never tried it, you could miss out on something really great"!

So from all of my experiance from all over the world I want to share some of my favorite places to eat and of course some of the ~~worst~~ worst".

"When you get Sour grapes, make Wine"

The View Rest.

One of my top favorite places to eat was at a place where I worked and had two night, two shows with Ronnie Milsap. The View Restaurant in Devils Lake, ND.

This was not only the biggest Lobster I had ever seen, much less eaten, in my life. I was expecting tough and dry and probably not fresh, after all we are in the heart of the Midwest, ND really? fresh seafood??

→

My drummer at that time told Harrassd
me to try it so I did.
After quite a while of waiting
and anticipating the 10 lb
lobster, it came out in
all its glory on a platter
that should serve a king.
Chef Charles himself walked
the beautiful orange beast
fully decorated to my
table. My mouth dropped to
the floor ~~and~~ as he sat him
down in front of me.
I proceeded to crack
his every part open ~~and~~
with my crackers and dip his
beautiful meat into hot
butter. There were others
at my table that I

shared my luscious lobster with but for the life of me, I can't remember which. I can tell you that was truly "the Best" Lobster I have ever eaten. Since then I have been back there twice. Each time is as wonderful as I remembered.

I'd highly recommend The View Restaurant for lobster. ✱✱✱✱✱ .

The Good Boy Band

HALE WHITE, TODD WOLSEY & JESSE WHITLEY

"STARVING ON THE ROAD. LIVING IT UP WITH
CATERING. NOT TOO APPEALING TO ME.
THEY WILL EAT ANYTHING!"

"EATING A GREAT COLD OYSTERS AT

SHUCHUMS IN PANAMA CITY BEACH, FL.

WE LOVE OUR OYSTERS!"

MARKET ST. JOHNS

MARCIA WILDER AND
KELLEY CORBITT

16

Market on The Warf

Now I was excited about this place!

We had a day off in the Port of St. John in Canada. We were so happy about a Meat & produce Market down by the Warf. Myself, Kelley and Marcia had a plan. We were gonna try some great local cheese and bread and some local wine and spend the evening in the room having a girls night.

We walked up and down this large market mid way and scoped my vendors goods. Finally, we settled

on a local Cheese Vendor
and bought some Port
Cheese. OK, our first
purchase bought, we moved
on to the wine next.
We ooh'd and ahh'd at
all the local Crafts and
such and finally we were
there at the Winery.
"Oh this is the best wine
in the world, people from
all over come here to buy
our wine" the nice lady
said. "However" we said.
I picked up a ~~bottle~~
what felt like any bottle
in that tiny space and
checked what kind and
the alcohol content of

sensable
Cork

each pretty bottle. Finally
arriving at a decision I
grabbed one up, set it on
the counter and asked
Kelly and Marcia if it
was ok and of course they
said, "We trust your judgement."
Bagged up and ready to
go we walked to the
end of the Market and
found a restaurant and
ate a dozen oysters but
thats another Chapter.
We finished and returned
to our individual rooms.
I put the Cheese in its
brown paper bag in the
frig in my room, set the
wine on the Counter and

ran a hot bubble bath.
We planned our girls
night in a few hours
later.
At 8:00 PM a knock at
my door told me it
was wine time. I opened
the door to my two
friends in their cozies
and glasses in hand.
We all plopped down
on the big bed and
proceeded to open and
pour the wine. OK I said,
it smells a little sweet
for me but who knows?
Taste it Kelly and see what
you think. By the look on
her face I could tell

it was no good. "Taste a like old sweet antique furniture" she said. Oh Hell, I knew we should've gotten a back-up. OK, OK. so lets try and enjoy it and open the cheese. ~~cheese~~ "BiG MiSTAKE" Smelt like Someone died a year ago and no one cared enough to bury them. I damn sure ain't eating anything that smells like that. I got two loud AMENs on that.

So needless to say our girls night was ruined by terrible antique smelling wine and "death cheese."

The Vending machines saved us

this night and I did
have someone run out to
local liquor Store and get
us a good bottle of wine.
We had fun, but I
do not recommend the
wine in Market in St. John
nor the Port Cheese. If you
buy either one make
Sure you can test taste
before buying.
"That's all I'm Sayin"

We kept the cool cash for
other wine bottles

400°'s Princess's

Now anyone who knows me at all is aware that I am a fanatic over Hot foods (spicy) especially spicy fried Hot Chicken. I've been eating this kind of chicken since I was at least five years old. I'm sure ~~not~~ ^(I ate it) as spicy as I eat it now, but still spicy.

My father George found a place one night back in the 1950's after playing the Opry at the Ryman Auditorium in Nashville. I'm almost ly litterally following his nose. They sent ~~took~~ took him to a brick-o-block building on Charlotte Ave. with 2 windows & two doors one in back + one in front

He walked in to the ~~smoke filled~~ Smoke filled establishment ~~only~~ with the smell that made his tounge water only to find he and he alone was the only white person in there. This ~~This~~ was some serious Soul food.

With about 4 wooden booths in the front the back room ~~of the~~ that had one long table ~~that~~ was designated for the White people. The stove had two large black cast iron skillets full of Hot lard bubbling over beautifully frying Chicken Breasts and quarters Legquarters to a ~~golden~~

Dark Golden Brown.

The man cooking the chicken ~~and~~ smiled up at my father and there was an instant friendship born. Bolton Polke was this distinguished black man's name. His wife sat behind the counter on a stool and ate the hot chicken and talked to the customers. My dad quickly became a regular and their biggest promoter of this great chicken. He even spoke of it on the gary occassionly and told folks to visit "The Chicken Shack" on Charlotte.

This chicken became a staple in our family over

Hot Chicken!

"I HAVE BEEN EATING THIS KIND OF CHICKEN
SINCE I WAS AT LEAST FIVE YEARS OLD."

400 DEGREES

−11−2017

人民共和国

RUSSIA

AUSTRALIA
IMMIGRA

GREAT
BRITAIN

×INDIA×

WITH MY FRIEND KENNY ORTEGA
WHO LOVES THE PAIN OF HOT CHICKEN

the next fifty some years.
Its made with dry
Cheyenne pepper, paprika,
white pepper and a few
secret ingrediants. Each piece
according to the heat you
like, or think you can endure,
is rolled in the mix of
all the ingrediants either
thick or not so thick and
then rolled and coated
with thick, white all
pourpose flour. Then fried to a
golden brown and placed
on two pieces of white bread
and topped with dill pickles
or, then wrapped in
wony paper and into to

a brown paper bag for
take out.
Scrumptous!!!
Rogo ~~don't be~~
Since "that night my dad
visited the Chicken Shack"
for the first time, it
has changed hands
quite a few times but
has pretty much stayed
in the same family
I personally opened my
own ~~resta~~ "Hot Chicken
Restaurant" back in the
early 2000's that was a
huge success but was
destroyed by divorce. "I
will open another"!! →

My favorite Hot Chicken Restaurants in Nashville are Prince's Chicken Shack on Edmondton off Dickerson Rd and ~~400 on 4th and~~ Slow ~~Peabody Downtown~~. on Myatt Dr. Burr

Now if you're expecting anything fancy you might as well forget it. You can eat in or take out. I like milk with mine so most of the time we take it home. Just a friendly hint, don't drink Carbonated drinks with this, it only makes it hotter. The pickles actually cool some of the heat down.

All of our closest friends
have become addicted to
the Chicken and at least
twice a week ~~see~~ ~~Randy~~ me
and ~~Randy~~ and our friends
~~go get~~ eat the Chicken
either on our boat or
out by a coz I fire outside
or at someone's kitchen table.
Afterwards there is always
a Euchre game!!
~~There be~~ I give this food
my highest score ★★★★★

(If you're lucky they'll make)
(you a Reuben sandwich)

2/00°
NAshville, TN

After my restaurant Hot Chickens.com
Closed down, one of our best Customers
opened her own very small Hot Chicken
restaurant not too far from our old
restaurant place.

I had heard from different
people that it was almost just
like ours was. Great reviews from
our old Customers. I had to
give it a try.

It was a teny little place with
one table inside. Very dark and dreary.
But that Chicken was expellant and
the aroma was just as great.

It wasn't located not in the best
part of town and I felt sorry
for the owner (Aqui) because I
Knew she needed to be Known
around Nashville for some of the
best Hot Chicken I had ever

eater. But once you get bit by the Hot Chicken bug, you'll go anywhere to get a piece.

We went there all the time, of course we got our orders to go as there was ~~just a~~ nowhere to set.

Finally Aqui bought her own building in a better part of town and ~~started~~ reconstructing it. During the reconstruction, she ~~served~~ prepared and served her Chicken out of a ~~food~~ truck she had bought ~~and~~ parked ~~in~~ in front of her building. We could only order to go but we didn't care, it was still the best in town.

After months & months of working alongside of her husban Jermain, the building was ready to open and Beat

and serve. "400° Hot Chicken."
The best in Nashville. 99% of
the Morgan family and friends
prefer this Chicken above all else
in Nashville. It always consistant
and Clean.

Many times when you see my
bus pull in town to town You
Can bet that there is a fridge
full of Mild to the hottest piece
Of Chicken ~~that is~~ You Can get.
It's my favorite thing to eat
after a Show!!

Aqui is an inspiration to a lot of
women who work and still manage
to be a mother and a wife.
"A True Success Story"
She sells a Shirt that says
"So Hot it'll Burn You Twice"
Amen
When

AQUI & LORRIE

Cap Juluca

Now this place is absolutely breathtakingly beautiful. Soft white sandy beaches and ~~with~~ crystal clear turquois waters. Which is exactly why we chose this hidden paradise to get married.

Our Villa faced the beautiful ~~Caribbean~~ Ocean ~~on~~ with a walkway from our door directly to the white sand and water. Truly Romantic and tranquil.

~~Unt~~ Like every other place we've gone, our first agenda was to find out the local eateries and

liquor stores. ~~and grocery~~
~~the~~

    The people of the island
~~are~~ were wonderful ~~and~~
~~and welcoming~~ and very
accomidating, not however
the greatest cooks. different
We tried so many local
cuisines and just couldn't
find one thing we really
liked. We kept dreaming
of how good our wedding
night meal was going to
be. We knew we were
headed for some great
lobster, Champaign, salad
                          But
until then we continued our
search for anything that

would satisfy our pallets.
No luck. From dried
goat, to strangely spiced
turtle soup to just plain
bland island favorites, what
ever that may be.

Finally the big day. It
was a beautiful day for a
beach wedding. Randy was
radiant and so handsome. I
couldn't believe how lucky
I was.

The preacher was a sweet woman
but not much of a peppy
soul.

A small arch facing the
aqua Caribean lined with
an array of fresh flowers awaited
me as I walked toward
$\longrightarrow$

Randy. Our Evening beach
Wedding was under way.
During the ceremony we poured
colored sand into a beautiful
glass vase that represented
our hearts combining to one.
After the ceremony we toasted
w/ champaign & a small-tiny
cake. Then signed the papers
and took tons of pictures.
While pictures were being
taken they were setting up
for a sunset dinner on the
beach. We were starving
and had been since we arrived
there. We just kept talking
about the lobsters that
were waiting for us.
    Finally, the tikki torches

were lit and we were
beckoned to our little table
with th a white table cloth
and Candles & flowers.

They poured us more Champaign
and served our first Course.
Salad. It was ok actually
but I could care less, "bring
me lobster".

Then we were served some
Kind of strange tasting
Soup. Not for me. I
think Randy ate it because
he was Starved.

Well after about an
hour and a half and My
now very dark outside except
the light of the Tikhi's, and
the wind becoming very

strong the lobsters arrived in 2 baskets. They opened the lids simultaniously and there they were, Two teeny spiny tailed lobsters, smoked?? or grilled?? I was devasted so was Randy althugh he acted very happy about our puny lobsters.

"Could we please have some butter for our lobsters"? I asked. "Sure mom" 30 mins later they brought our butter, in pats!!!

Cap Juluca is beautiful but could not get food satisfied for nothing. I will start carrying a bottle of ghost pepper sauce on tobassco sauce")

One night we were so hungry we hailed a cab to the local grocery store. Tiny, Tiny, Tiny. We were in search of ~~some~~ some comfort food bad.

We found some ground beef & Tomato juice and a little salt & pepper & believe it or not some chili pepper and one big onion. We also got a single sleeve of crackers. We were so happy. We got back to the room and guess what? No pot to cook it in and the maids quarters where they fix our breakfast was closed up. :(

Randy went out side to find a maid for our bungalo and low and behold, he found one.

Although sceptical, she agreed to let us in her little kitchen. OMG, all that was in there was a tiny refrigerator, a small sink & counter and a tiny, tiny hot plate to cook our Chili. OOps, we did not get a knife to cut the onion. Thank God she had one, ha would not cut a stick of butter. But we sliced and diced until our hands were sore. Although starved and sore hands, we were having a blast showing the Island women how to make American Chili. Drinking wine and Champaign was our saving grace for as long as it was taking to cook the beef and onions on one small Hot plate. Felt like hours.

Finally it was done. The island ladies loved it!! We cleaned up our mess while waiting for the Chili to cook So when it was done, We ~~found~~ Could go to our bungalo and pig out. We did just that. With open doors to the skirt of the Ocean and Candles lit, we sat ~~eat~~ in our bungalo and ate the best Chili ever. Well at least since we'd been there. Not the greatest ~~food there~~. But a heavenly place to go to relax and be with one another. Just take

Some hidden away food!

AVO – Nashville

Gag – I can't tell you how unflavored, and unappetizing the meal was.

The Restaurant itself was very cool and very LA looking (for whatever that's worth). I wasn't aware what poor Veegans go thru. This was a tortuous meal for me other than the company. My produce and two of managers my dear friends. We laughed thank God and got through. I have a pic of this meal, and I still don't enjoy the meal even from far away.

No flavor what so ever. It was kind of sad because

the servers were very nice.
I left and stopped at
Krystals and ate a ~~Che~~
Krystal Chick Sandwich.
You Can always count on
Krystal to serve it up
Hot and good! Yummy
~~Next up New York City~~ '

"TUFF WHITLEY AND PRESTON COOK LOVE MEXICAN FOOD!"

RANDY WHITE

Rosepepper Cantina

last night

The best mexican food I've had maybe ever.

Joined by my husband Randy son Jesse, daughter in law Ashlee and our friends Kimbery & Darryl Worley.

3 different kinds of great salsa from hot med & mild. all were excellent. Chips were superb. Cheese dip was limp hot and delish.

I don't normally drink margaritas and I had two top shelf and they were OMG great.

Tyler we ordered the Sonoma Enchilads. Green Chili (almost as good as mine)

smothered with cheese
and two fried eggs. Side
of refried beans & rice.
I shoveled my food in ~
because I'd been on a
low carb diet so I'm
not sure if it was really
that awsome or just
starved for weeks.
Either way, great vibe
and company.
Highly recomend this.
The Owner Ernie Chaisson
was a dear friend of mine.
He passed away in 2014
from Cancer.
R.I.P. Ernie

"   "

"It's hard sometimes to tell
the truth about really bad
restaurants because most of
the time it's really not the
server's fault. But its someones
so the truth is the truth

"Best Salad of Life"
Toronto Airport

Endive lettuce, raddish,
Cucumber, miniture pickles, Celery
& pork belly topped with fried
Soft boiled egg!!!
This was a total surprise of
greatness, in an airport none the
less. Toronto Airport. I can't
remember the exact name of

the restaurant but I'll never forget it and I will always go back for the abundant tastes of in one salad. It was a great way to end the trip. and Everyone experienced a great meal from the burgers to shrimp to great beer on draft.

Moncton NB
Like the residue on the ~~inside~~ inner
~~can~~ can lining of an exposed
Vienna sausage - Scrambled Egg

Caserio   The Centre
NB   @ Caserio New Brunswick
                     Italies Classic
                          Line

(Catch 22)
This was an awful breakfast
But we had a great
laugh. Here are some
pics from the moment.

                    Continued

Montego Bay
Wendover, NV

Was somewhat nervous to
try the great looking large
Crossands at the Casino however,
Dale White was eager to test
them for two days. Finally
on our way out to leave
for Salt Lake City Utah to fly
home, he broke down and used
his last food voucher to
purchase two. One for me and
one for him.
As I slipped in the van
to leave, in the back seat
Dale was deep into his
second bite. "How ~~was~~ is it
I said"?
His discription was priceless!

" Hales Comment

It's pretty good. On a scale of 1-5, it gets a five for appearance and texture, and a 3 for taste because of a lack of buttery flavor (no grease).

It has interwoven flakes that are collapsable much like an accordion". He ate them both.

The ~~two~~ low taste rating did not deter his appetite. Over all the rating was good.

The ~~esp~~ engraploury texture help to over ride the flaws of taste.

To close, I did have one bite

HALE WHITE

"TRAVELIN' ALONG,
SINGIN' MY SONG"

Belize, San Pedro

I had to do a show in
Belize. Just my accoustic
show. I couldn't wait.
Randy was flying down a few
days later to meet me. Until
then I familarized my self
with this quaint lil' island.
My girlfriend at the time
and her husband and me
and Randy shared a condo on
the waters edge. Our friends
Jeff and Pam owned the
Condo and that who I was
doing the show for. Randy
finally arrived and in true
San Pedro style we got in
our golf cart and drove
down middle Rd. to the

airport to get him. There
are only to three streets
there, Front, middle, and
back.

People were so friendly!
Were too long away from
my Hot Chicken so I decided
to go the only grocery store
and got all the ingredients
for my Hot Chicken.

We told the whole Condo
Community we were making
Hot Chicken that night.
They were all waiting in
anticipation as we cooked
away in the Condo. Of
Course we were drinking
Wine, watching the sunset
and laughing.

We formed a line at the Kitchen Counter where the Chicken was done, each one having their own spefic job for preparing the Chicken. One put the Chicken on the bread from the Skillet, one put the pickles on, one wrapped them in wax paper, and one stacked them on top of each other. Time to deliver to the hungry waiters. We did just that. Everyone loved it and so did We.

Just an added note person
The Greenbay Airport made
me throw away my
store packaged Van Heussen
pickle ☺. Never had even
been open. I did not like those
people

Just or another note - Alaskan
Air have the nicest flight
attendants!

Zen
Juneau, Alaska

Great Thom Ka Kai Soup
Highly recommend the Crispy Duck!
The View Restaurant
North Dakota
The best lobster Ever

"MY DAUGHTER MORGAN WITH A BEACH BALL STOMACH"

Alaska

So we were there for
five days. Each day we
searched for fresh oysters
on the half shell. Every
town, every restaurant, No
One had them, "Come on"
its alaska — Cold water etc...
Five shows in a row ~~is~~ and
I'm needing a fix.

Finally The last night
after my final show
We came across a place
Called Humpty's. Randy
asked if they had raw oysters
and by Gosh, they did. We
asked them if The Could do
Oyster shooters, they did not
Know how. So Randy asked

if he would come around
the bar and make them.
they were so nice
There were six or seven of
us. Me & Randy, my friend
Kelly, Marcia, Jeff, Mark
and someone else I can't
remember.
Finally my recipe for
Oyster Shooters were served:
   Oyster in Shot glass
   Dolop of Cocktail Sauce
   pinch fresh horseraddish
   Drop of Woosterchin
   Tabasco to taste
   add great Vodka
   Then Shoot all at once

We were ready.

All holding our glasses up in the air toasting a very successful trip. 1, 2, 3 Cheers.

Ug ..... 😖 I'm choking on my oyster. It's not moving for what seemed like eternity. Finally Randy jumped up and lifted my arms and pushed in on my back and out it popped. Duh..., I had just finished my fifth and final show so my throat was swollen and tensed up. I was lucky to swallow spit let alone an oyster. I looked over

at my friend who was
crying afraid I was
dying. I got up and
hugged her.
So much fu
Alashar Oystus :)

"MY SISTERS, LIANA, DRINKING OYSTER SHOOTERS!!!"

Gonzales, LA.

Mama's Southern Tradition
Restaurant.
Advertising — Cat Head
Biscuits.
We had to go. I love Cat
Head Biscuits.
Dale my Piano player
had never heard of such.
I assured him that they
were awesome.
If my memory serves
me correct, and I think
it does. We all ordered
Biscuits. Some with gravy
some not.
I laughed so hard when
Dales order came out. First of

All it was Nothing like
the picture on the menu.
We'd ordered a Top sirloin
steak on a CAT HEAD Biscuit.
the steak was the size of
a damn quarter. The biscuit,
normal size yet Hard.
We called the waitress over
who was also the owner and
showed her the picture on
the menu then what
was on his plate. We said
"these are nothing alike" at
which time, she admitted
it look nothing like the
picture. So she said let
me go back to the Kitchen
and fix it at which point
Dale said no, no, its ok

"I just based my whole order off the picture".
She went to the kitchen anyway and brings back another piece of steak the same size as the first one. Needless to say, we all fell out on the floor laughing.
"We Wont Go Back"

"The steak was overwhelmed by the "~~smale~~ biscuit"."

Monkton, Pa
New Brunswick

~~Cassie~~: The Centex

You must now that my
Piano player Nate White is
serious about his food from
texture to smell to presentation.
So going to eat with him on
the broad road is quite an
experience.

I have pictures here
depicting how terrible my,
Ashlie, Ric and Mike's
breakfast was. totally unbearable.
The sausage links we like
something I had never eaten.
Weird seasoning and meat.
No one could eat it.
So in walks Nate and

"LIKE THE RESIDUE ON THE INNER LINING OF AN
EXPIRED VIENNA SAUSAGE CAN" - HALE WHITE

from a far we all watch
him walk around scanning
the breakfast bar.
So finally he come to our
~~se~~ table and sets down
with a huge plate of food.
"Not one thing looked
desirable." He felt safe
in getting a ~~to~~ Crossant
at least on the side.
Huge mistake! Kale is
a Crossant Conasur!!!
He could not eat the
bacon which was floppy
and dripping of grease
and here ~~is list description~~
~~of the Crossant.~~ how he assessed
the morning Crossant "The problem
with this Crossant is, it is not

soft enough, And the future looks like a piece of white bread. By Contrast, a proper Croissant Series of inner ~~feature~~ ~~is~~ ~~with~~ woven flakes that are collapsable and ~~springing~~. Springy." Unlike microple wholes in this one."

Also He had some refried beans on the side — "Lm—" First Mistake— Do not eat mexican food in Moncton, New Brunswick." Nale described this taste ~~as~~ compared to "The residual liquid on the inner lining of a Vienna sausage Can".

Blue Water Rest
in St. John.

This was a great atmosphere and cool hang.

Jesse and I set out to get some mussels that I had told him was some of the best, if not the best I'd ever had last time we were here. The place I'd eaten before we could not feind. So we were taken to Blue Water. Great service and watching Jesse take it all in was awesome. However the mussels left a lot to be desired. They were dry and while displayed beautifuly, there wasn't any juice or real taste. The great surprise was, Jesse & I

ordered Tuna Tar Tar. - OMG
the best. It was in a
beautiful bowl, garnished
well. layered with avocado
then tuna and repeated.
A new favorite of mine
in St. John. ☆☆☆☆

Señor Burritos
Lakewood CO.

If you know me at all
you know how much I
love green Chili. We stopped
here after a long day of
flying. We were all starving
and mexican food sounded
great to all of us.

The decor and building
left a lot to be desired. The
service wasn't great and the
green Chili wasn't green at
all. But one bite and Daisy
my background singer/guitar player
Were hooked. (I love that she
likes hot spicy food like I do.)
Colorado makes great Green
Chili I don't know where
this dish originated but

my family has eaten it
for years and of course
make our own. "The Best"
~~Thos~~ Senor Burritos is
worth the stop if you're
passing through. I recommend
a Green Chili & Cheese
Quesidilla.
Olé

Señor Burritos II
53 N. Kipling • Lakewood
For take-out orders, call
202-1185

Joe's Crabshack
on Daytona Beach.

From a distant it looked
very promising at a late
Hour.

We were all seated in
a large rectangular room
is right on the ocean.
The whole band and I
and little Grandson Tuff.
It was very late and I
know the staff was tired, I
guess the Cook was too.

I ordered Crab legs and what
seemed forever, they finally
Came out. Edward described
them as "having the Consistancy
of a Twizzler". I could not
even break them.

No one's meal was good.
Don't Go there.

OUR COMBINED OBSESSION WITH VIETNAMESE
CUISINE INSPIRED US TO CRAFT OUR OWN HATS!

"WHEN WE HAD OUR FIRST EGG MY WHOLE FAMILY
WAS CALLED AS IF A GRANDCHILD WAS BORN."

Our Chickens & Eggs

When We moved to our little 5 acre farm, Randy and I wanted to have our own Chickens and Rooster for fresher Eggs. When we had our first egg my whole family was called as if a grandchild was born. We raised these babies since they were 2 weeks old. Now they are so big and funny and giving us great Eggs.

This picture was when they were about 5 months, not ~~eating~~ laying eggs yet.

Rooster is Hustoff, Biggest Hen is Claura, then Elsie, Mrs Howell, then little Pidgie. My mom named them and went with us to pick them out. Of Course they gravitate to Randy as we Call him Noah.

Here are are a couple of pictures of dishes I made with our eggs & veggies from our garden.

Annapolis MA

"   "

"Great rile frod place"
Sevcie was eptremely slow
We went for breakfast.
We started off with a wonderful
Baked cherry tomatoes & Cheese
dish and great toast flats.
Warm & tastey. Now I
Ive l一 pate', so I ordered
appitzer small l一 pati
Sandwiches. Well they put
really seedy Strong mustard
on it pickled yellow peppers
& onions. I ate only a bit
and that was enough for
me.
For my main Course I
ordered Something different

that I'd never tried before.
Why would I ever think
about ordering this? I don't
know.
OK here goes:
       Baked lima beans (that
turned out to be Butter Beans)
with some kind of sweet sauce
on top. Then two fried
Eggs on top. On top of that,
& a thick layer of Crunchy
Sprinkles of garlic toast. Too!!
Garlicy and I love garlic.
    Terrible Breakfast.
Daisy my guitar player/BGV
played it safe and ordered
3 poached eggs. However she
waited thirty mins to get
it. ★ Then ordered
a piece of toast
& that took
30 mins
as well. The coffee wasn't
that great
as well.
★ Either

Oslo, Norway.

After a long long night of travel and customs, finally we were inside the huge airport with great shops and restaurants.

Randy and the band and I walked up and down the hallways trying to find the perfect meal after a long flight.

Finally, Randy, myself, Daisy and Kai found a local fresh fish marked Restaurant. OMG!!! It was great. Small shrimp on top of mayo on wheat Bread. Boiled egg and avocado mixed in. With dill on side of the dish.

No. 21

They also had great sushi to choose from and many other beautiful shrimp & Crab dishes. Seems like European Countries still take pride in their food and ~~services~~ service.

☆☆☆☆☆

"I WAS SO FULL THAT KAI HAD TO CARRY ME OUT."

Puerto Varta

Randy and I and Pam Tillis and Matt Spicher took a great trip to the beautiful city by the Gulf. A total King and Queen resort. The pool, the snorkling, the beach were majestic as were the mountains peaking up from the water just minutes away by kyaking.

The resturant when we performed was surrounded by the splashing gulf against the windows.

Every day we all had our personal butler who would come and prepare breakfast and serve us all

delicious fruits, eggs, Crossant &
Champaign in our indidulual
villas.

Every day the men of the
resort would Climb the
mountains behind the resort
and bring down many large
Coconuts.

They would Carve out the
Coconuts and serve us rum
drinks in the beautiful pool.
Randy told them every day to add
all the white liquor they could
find. They never Could get him
drunk.

One day they brough us as a
snack, fresh cut up Coconut
and different dipping Sauces to
dip in.

One was my personal favorite.
Brushed Habenero Sauce —
OMG. I ate so much,
and enjoyed great praton
tequila in my Coconut for
drink.

Our last night there
we were invited to a huge
castle like home a top a
mountain behind the Resort.
This place was monsterous.
The patio/veranda was
unclosed half way up by
a thick glass. You could see
for miles. There was also
a fire in a pit by a seating
area by the glass.
This was our final night
to really enjoy ourselves.

We went in to a huge round stone & glass table where we set down to an authentic Tequilla Tasting. "I was in Heaven." Then we were served great steaks, salads and Sorbet and a coconut Ice cream.

After all was said and done we were served Brandy on the patio along with some great Cigars.

Overlooking the gulf from our view, The owner gave us all a two way radio to hold. At the Count of 3 we all said "~~Ariva, Ariva~~ Arriva Arriva and a huge

display of fireworks went
off for at least 10 min
over the ocean. Just for
us.
   We all teared up
and will remember this
night forever.
        " Gracias "
              Omego's

Well be back

P.S. Great Chips & Guacomole
                    ⊙ / olé

     ⨉⨉⨉⨉⨉

"The Omni Hut"

One of my favorite places to
eat.
Located just east of Nashville
in Smyrna Tn.
This is a Polynessian Restaurant
that my dad George used to
take all of his family to
eat. He is the one who
introduced all of his kids
to the different foods of the
world.
This was as close to Hawaii
we had ever seen.
The hut is all wicker and
Rope Balls hanging all over.
There are remenents of
their previous trips to the
Big Island. One room is

lit with all Black light and plastic flowers that light up so brighley on the walls. Fish tanks as well are all lit. Polynessian music plays and the women wear muu muu dresses and are very Cultural.

The food is impecable. I recommend the Rumaki with "Hot mustard". The Poo Poo Platter with a little ~~sm~~ tiny Grill. In grilling your steak on a stick. Also Has rib Tid Bits & Egg rolls. Serves 4. My dish I love to get is Chicken Chow Mein a staple there.

It's a great social place to eat.
But be sure to bring your own liquor or wine! It's a dry County.

⭐⭐ ⭐⭐⭐

WITH LINDA AND RON CHANCEY

Lobsters from Main

During Fall

Every year our Best friends Mike & Sheila Willis and Randy and I order Lobsters, oysters & Cavier from Maine; Play Euchre and drink great Scotch & Wine. They have a beautiful farm of about 130 acres in Tennessee and we spend the weekend there and Eat, drink, pray & be merry. Randy and Mike partake in some great cigars and S. Sheila and just talk under our blankets & drink wine.

The morning after is awesome as well with Country Ham, Flowers Sausage, A place in White Creek Tn that packages their own sausage. And one of my favorite Sausages ➔

Mayos. Its been a staple in
the Mugan family for years.
So we eat breakfast, play
a little more Euchre, ~~Euchre~~
Drink Coffee and we go home.
Sometimes this great
gathering happens in Maine. One
of favorite places to go as a
Couple group.

JESSE WHITLEY AND HALE WHITE

Salutoget

Helsinki, Finland   Scandanvian Bistro

This was suggest to all of us,
in the Band. Hale of Course found
it and it came highly recomended.
We walked in to a very European
and glamorous place, but people
were dressed casual so we felt at
home. We had traveled the day
to get there and all of our appitites
were ~~very~~ at the top the menu list
to satisfy.
The restaurant used to be a
_____ and was extremely
Reverant.
We met and were served by the
manager Simon. The service
and his people skills were
impecable.

Randy

The ladies were placed our orders
first. Daisy for an appetizer ordered
(1) a single Oyster with onion &
vinegar sauce for 10€ And a local Beer
Our main course was Finland's
favorite - Salmon Soup. I ordered
a glass of Cab wine (of Cruise)
and Escargo for an appetizer for
me and Randy. Ran was a little
leary as he had never tried them.
For my main Course I ordered
Pan seared Lobster. I'm
unsure of every ones order but
Kai ordered pan seared Scallops
& Shrimp. And ordered this
terrible smelling, smoky so
tasting burnt like Whisky. Oh
God I took one drink and

just about gagged. UGH ∵
(Randy & I bought his birtbday
dinner).
Ric ordered some small
little crunchy fish like
looking Sardines + mashed
potatoes. My Randy had been
craving a good ole steak. So
that was his order.
   The bread was served with
real butter that we all
wanted to just keep eating.
Real Honest to goodness)
Butter and real Cream
Farm to table. (I was so
happy)
   The escargot came first
and of course I made Ran)
try it. It was dripping

in Golden Butter with a thin
Cheese as well and garlic.
Randy Said "Had he known
Snails were this good, he would
have cooked them on the sidewalk
when he was little" LoL.
Truly the best I do ever eaten.
We were only a few blocks from
our beautiful hotel and the air
was crisp so it all made
for a great Week Back.

Then as dinner was ending I was ~~app~~
approached by a gentleman who Priests
walked up to our table and ever
politely said "Excuse Me, but we,
my friends and I noticed you
were wearing a scapula!" →

fr those who don't know – its a "Catholic thing". – Look it up. Turns out they were four priests celebrating their 50 anniversary as Catholic priests. They said they were proud of me showing my Catholic faith. We prayed together and said our Goodbyes. My Mother was so happy when I told her about the Priests.

+

☆☆☆☆

great Butter!"

"MY MOTHER WAS
SO HAPPY WHEN I
TOLD HER ABOUT
THE PRIESTS"

"THE BREAD WAS SERVED WITH REAL BUTTER
THAT WE ALL JUST WANTED TO KEEP EATING."

So my guitar player Todd Woolsey (The horse eater) told us a story one day while we were riding the bus about when he was a little boy and the family outings they would take when he was a little boy.

He told us of how his dad who was a preacher, would take him and his brother and sisters for Sunday drives. This was a big day for the Woolsey family. They were not a rich family by any means but were very very frugal. He told us how his dad would drive them to the ice cream store and they would all run in and his dad would stand them in front of all the delicious flavored and colored ice cream and tell them, "Now IF you could have an ice cream, which one would you choose?" The hard and I were almost in tears as he proceeded to tell us that they would all pick what they would choose if they could afford it and all would leave empty handed."

We were devasted for Todd. So everywhere we went that had ice cream we all offered to buy Todd one a cone.

He later explained that he and his brother and sisters thought it was fun and his father was just trying to keep them excited about what was to come in their lives.

In Burlington Vt. Todd asked if on our way out of town, if we could stop at the Original Ben & Jerry's Ice cream parlor, of course we all said yes

We even made phone calls to people who knew the story of Todd (my son Jesse for one,) that we were taking Todd to get icecream at the Oregon Ben & Jerrys.

Fun day watching Todd enjoy his ice Cream. :)

A Hunting We Will Do

When I was a little girl my
dad was my everything and everything
he did is etched in my mind
forever. He loved food, friends,
Card playing, family and hunting
and fishing. Hunting was his
favorite. It brought him together
with his best friends like Stuey Bears,
Grandpa Jones, T Tommy ~~Cut~~ Cutrer
and of course a family priest.
He never hunted big game like
deer and such, he thought they
were too beautiful. But what he
did hunt assuredly we would
eat for dinner that night.
Dad would bring home anything
from squirrel, Rabbit ~~or~~ to pheasant.
Take them to the picnic table out
back to clean and prepare them
to be cooked. Thats ~~why~~ mom

Came in. In the Kitchen she would make squirrel or Rabbit gravey and fry up (just like Chicken) The squirrel or Rabbit. It was always a feast of some kind when dad was home.

Me personally, I did not care for Squirrel or Rabbit. I just ate it to be with dad and my family. My brother Marty still makes these rodent dishes Lol and I still do not partake.

Sorry about my writing but I'm often on the bus reding and the roads are ~~all~~ very bumpy.

:(

favorite pastime.

New York City

Kelly, Marcia, Jeff and I
had a few days off in NYC so
I decided I would treat them
to a little "taste" of my favorite
Caviar bar. Just a taste because
they had never had great
Caviar, if ever they'd had caviar
So I had set aside an extra
$500.00 Cash to treat them to
a "taste"! At that time of my
life the money was tight, so
$500 meant a lot.
    I had been to the Caviar bar
years ago with my manager
Tony Conway and my assistant
DeAnn Ballentine. That was a
a beautiful night at the height
of my eating experience.

Years later after a drought
of hits and money, I was
working again and finally
making some decent money. So
it was a night of celebration.

There is a doorbell on
a small skinny door on the
street in NYC. Ring the bell,
they buzz you up and seat you
in a very exclusive dining
area over looking the beautiful
City of New York.

We were so excited and ready
to laugh and eat one of
my favorite extravagant
treats.

The waiter brings me the
menu. The menu with NO prices
on it. :(

But I knew Caviar and I
knew just what to order my
friends. Problem was, how
much?? Um?
Well, wanting to look like I
knew what I was doing, I
ordered what I thought
was about $150.⁰⁰ of Caviar.
So we ordered some great Russian
Vodka, a must with great
Caviar along with the
~~toast~~ blini, and fiche.
Finally here it came...
the big moment.
The Caviar bowl was only as
big as a bowl of cereal, and
we dove in like starving Vultures.
There wasn't a morsel left
and Kelly bought the last

Shots of Vodka for everyone. For that
moment We were living high and
happy and living the good
life.

Then Came the bill!
Of course it was delivered
to me. "whoever" I looked at the
bill and thought I was
seeing double! $14,500.00 !!!,
I gasped and immediatly
started crying hysterically,
Jumping around like
a fool, Actually, Screaming.
We were all ~~it in~~ in a
disarray and saw a jail sentence
in our futures.
Oh God what do I do,
Who Can help me? The
writer, also the ~~mait~~ Maitre d'

~~was~~ sweating and cussing in what sounded like "Tongues" I did Not have the funds to pay!

My friends were in a panic. I finally Called a dear friend in PCB and as I was trying to talk through my tears, I ~~blurted~~ blurted out " I need $~~$4,500~~4,500". I heard him scream " WHAT". I told him of my situation and if he would Just please put the bill on ~~the~~ his Card I swear I'll have it in his account first thing Monday morning after I work.

Thank God he trusted me and he asked to speak to

the manager.
As we all huddled up in tears. The manager came over & and handed me the phone. It was my friend in Fla who said "It's all taken care of so quit crying." We all hugged and got out of there as fast as we could. Happy and walking down the street in New York I decided it was a good idea to get a tattoo to remind me "Don't get above your raising". My tat says Gi Gi which is what my grandchildren call me.
Thanks friend in Fla

By the way
          450 gms
is not $1,450.00 in Caviar
... it's $4,500.00 !!

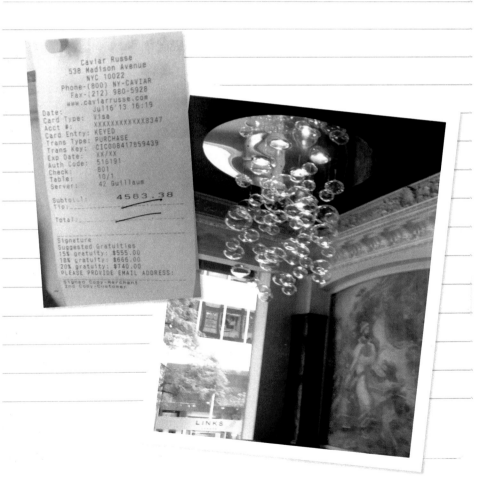

```
            Caviar Russe
          538 Madison Avenue
               NYC 10022
        Phone-(800) NY-CAVIAR
          Fax-(212) 980-5928
         www.caviarrusse.com
Date:           Jul16'13 16:19
Card Type:      Visa
Acct #:         XXXXXXXXXXXXX8347
Card Entry:     KEYED
Trans Type:     PURCHASE
Trans Key:      CIC008417859439
Exp Date:       XX/XX
Auth Code:      516191
Check:          801
Table:          10/1
Server:         42 Guillaum

Subtotal:         4583.38
Tip:_____

Total:_____

Signature
Suggested Gratuities
15% gratuity: $555.00
18% gratuity: $666.00
20% gratuity: $740.00
PLEASE PROVIDE EMAIL ADDRESS:

Signed Copy-Merchant
2nd Copy-Customer
```

LINKS

Devels Lake N. D
The View

First of all, I love this place. Its
a great Venue to work. I
was playing with Ronnie Milsap of
whom I love.
The resteraunt was upstairs
above the Show room.
After the show the band and
I decided to splurge and go
this very nice and quite pricing
Resturaunt. My drummer at that time
Howard Mayberry suggested I order
the Lobster, "In North Dakota?"
I thought he was insane. "You
don't order seafood out in N. D.
But against my better judgement
I ordered it. Not just it, but
a 10 lb Lobster to boot.

Everyone knows you don't order that big of a lobster. I was told "the bigger the lobster the tougher the meat".

Well not too long after I ordered the Kitchen doors sprang opened and out walked the Chef Carrying my 10 lb lobster on a silver platter. He was setting on top a bed of beautiful Green lettuce and lemon slices all around him.

All of our eyes were opened bigger than saucers! ☺

If presentation is everything this was the "Crem da la crem".

I was given my Crackers to get into the giant monster and I lit into it.

All eyes were on me and my "Lobbie". Of course I shared, what do you think I am? We all ate on that Lobbie for at least an hour.

I was covered in lobster juice and butter as was the rest of my party.

Truly the best Lobster I have ever eaten. I've been back a couple of times and continue to order the same thing anytime.

I can say it was the absolute ultimate meal.

The View ☆☆☆☆☆

"MINE AND RANDY'S
NEW YEAR'S EVE
RITUAL – CAVIAR AND
ALL THE FIXINGS."

New Years Eve

This is what Randy and I do
evry New Years Eve. Either just us
two, or our friends Mike & Sohaila.
I order some beautiful Caviar
from Petrossian with all of the
garnishes. Randy buys some great
PINK Champaign (my favorite).
And if we're alone we eat and
drink and toast in the bed
most of the time with our dogs
Wuzzy & Puddin'. Then the dogs
go to bed and we try to
bring in the New Year Correctly
and romantecly. Any way it
turns out is Wonderful

☆☆☆☆☆

Genes Oyster Bar
Panama City, Fl.

The Absolute best ever!!

My dad taught me at an early age
how to detect a great oyster. He
taught me about many foods, but
oysters are my most memorable food
with dad - except for Hot Chicken.
   I believe Genes is the oldest Oyster
Bar in Panama City. Over 50 yrs.
I had the pleasure of meeting
Gene about 5 years ago. His
wife & sister in law ran the place.
Gene passed away in 2016, but
his restaurant is still run by his
wife. This place is in total
disguise. It tucked away in a
residential area on the east

end of Panama City. It seats
about 20 people (maybe)
maybe less. The oyster Shuckers
stand before you and Shuck
your oysters. They also have
the best oyster Stew, (next to
mom's). :)
They serve a baked oyster with
Cheese & Jalapeno pepper & butter
that is to die for.
They have shrimp etc. But
all the locals go for those
great Oysters. I go there
eny time I go to Panama City.
Which is where my heart wants
to retire.
                    "Just saying"

☆ ☆ ☆ ☆ ☆

"WEEZY ALWAYS TRYING TO GO WITH ME"

A Beautiful Dessert

This great desert was in a little fishing town in Norway. Eaten by Lyndsy our tour manager on our seas.

Flaky cookie crunch set in between two mounds of a beautiful homemade cream surrounded by berries. Raspberries, Strawberries & Cloud berries. Cloudberries are a beautiful tasting fruit. I have only seen in Norway. The dish is topped with Basil. A beautiful desert.

My Randy tried Whale in Norway for the first time. He begged me to taste, but I'm too sentimental. He said it was good but now that he has tried it, he said "that git for whale". "I'm glad". Gave me the willies, "Not the Free Willy's". Ame

Not for Me

"The best "Salad of Life""

Helsinki.
        In a little Cafe on
a great street in a really
Cool shopping district Randy
and I came across this
little place full of pastries,
Sandwiches, fruit, Cheese, olives
you name it, this place had a
little of Everything.
        Randy ordered a Cheese
pastry pastry and a Cappacino.
I ordered a great salad with
fresh lettuce, Cucumber, fresh
motzerella Cheese, Cherry tomatoes and
a mound of fresh tuna salad
and a Cressant. Seriously
the Best I've ever had. Over

Soporos Sushi
Gallatin, Tn.

One of our favorites. The fish
is fresh and Danny the
owner is always wearing
a smile. His servers are
polite, funny and quick.
The Sushi Chefs are brilliant
and tastiful.
    It is about 15 min from
our home which beats the
Hell out of Nashville Traffic.
    I seriously reccomend
~~Suppros~~ in Gallatin, TN.
Saporos

Jesse loves it!!
    That is all His LOL

            A A A A

Slaw Burn
Hot Chicken
Madison, Tn.

A great Hot Chicken place.
They serve more than just
Chicken.
  Livers
  Barbeque
  Turnip greens
  White Beans
  Baked Beans
my favorite fried Okra - Spicy or Not
  Fried Pickles
  and much more.
These folks are Kind and
friendly and cook great.
  Service with a Smile
    ☆☆☆☆☆

Shuckums, Panama City.

We have been going to PC since Morgan was about 3 or 4 yrs old. Shuckums was a favorite from the first time we ate there. Now my grandchildren love it. They eat the Crablegs, we adults eat the oysters. Sandy told them how we like our oyster shooters, now its a ritual when we are there, we stop a couple times a week just for the shooters. Here is the recipe if you want to try.

In a shot glass:
1 med fresh oyster
1 shot of your choice Vodka

1 t of Cochtail Sauce
1/2 t Horseraddish-Fresh
1/2 t. woosterchire
2 drops tobasco.

1, 2, 3, Shoot!
    Swallow whole

JESSE WITH KIDS

MY SISTERS LIANA, BETH AND CANDY

Boston, MA

One day I flew into Boston
before the band because I
didn't want the long bus
ride.
When I arrived I ~~went fro~~
hailed a taxi from the airport
to my hotel. There, I freshened
up and decided to get another
Cab to take me to a great
local oyster / seafood Bar.
Americans Oldest Restaurant;
Union Oyster House! I felt that
slipped back in time to
a bar that slanted forward
from years of use, truly a
historic Boston Bar.
By myself I sat down at
the bar to the nicest

Oyster shucker / Bartender ever.
The people seated around
me, where from different
places all over the
U.S. Very nice people.
It was just me this night
all by myself and loving it.
I started with a glass of
white Rhisling wine and
a bowl of Clam Chowder —
The best ever in life.
Then my friend "The Shucker"
began Shucking me succulent
Raw East Coast oysters. With
fresh Horseraddish, Cocktail
Sauce & Tobasco Sauce. I ate
so many, I lost track.
All of a Sudden my Shucker
friend bring out about a

20lb lobsta. Said, "Any one went some of Larry the Lobstr? Of Course, I wanted it, but I refrained. This was one of the best nights I'd spent with only me (Barree) in years.

I ♥ Boston

Chesepeak Bay
Chestertown, MD

One of my favorite places to
stay and enjoy the waters of
the Bay.

I'm always invited to stay
at a beautiful estate on the Bay.
By myself in this beautiful
home overlooking the bay. I
just walk about 100 yds and I
set on the sand as the waves
come up to greet me. I walk
awhile and collect sea glass, green,
blue, orange, all colors. Of Cause
I turn my music on Rod McQuen
"The Sea" I usually stay
down by the waves for a couple
of hours then gather my sea
glass and walk back to the

house. On the way there I stop at the pool and set with my feet dangling in the cool water. Then to the house for my nap before the show.

When I wake up the sun is setting on the Bay and I can't believe the beauty of this place.

I hear noises coming from somewhere in the house.

It Pam Tillis, there to get her shower for the show. She does her own agenda when we go there, but we meet up to get ready for our show.

We get picked up by two seperate vehicles as we both carry way too much luggage.

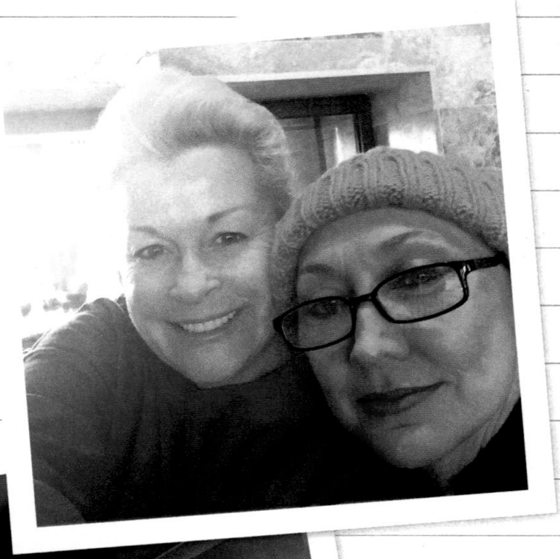

Better to have than to have not.
We are performing at a
great marina outside on
the bay. It's like playing in
heaven to me. The audience
brings their chairs at find
their place in the sand close
to the waves.
After the show we are
treated to great, fresh, spicy
Crabs cooked right there.
I'm in heaven there.
One of my most favorite
places to be and perform.

Snooze AM Restaraunt
Phoenix Az.
Az University

Jesse Kith, Hale White and I
wondered around for a great
place to eat that morning.
Ha!, We found it.
We sat outside on this
beautiful day.
Now Hale is one who wants to
know how everything is prepared,
real butter? real Dairy products?
Are the Crossants made with Collapable
interwoven flakes? so on & so on
So doesn't matter where we are
you must figure at least a
10 min order from Hale. Very
entertaining. After we all
ordered Soon our food came

out and was beautiful.
Nate ordered a Reuben sandwich
with slaw on it on a pretzel bun
and Crispy hashbrowns, and
Chocolate pancakes, coffee &
fresh squized pulp orange juice!
Jesse and I had eggs
Benedict mine with arugula
on top his with out. We
also had Crispy Hashbrowns
and a bottle of Tabassco.
Great place
✰ ✰ ✰ ✰ ✰

Crawfish Boil

When we lived on the lake we used to have people over all the time either to swim or boat or eat.

One of my favorite things we did was have an annual Crawfish boil.

Joy Holder who used to work with me was from Louisianna. He and I loved Craufish

We would play in show in LA and bring home 90 lbs of Crawfish and invite all the folks in we lived.

Joy would come and set up all the boilers and spices and of course bring our Craufish he brought back from Lousianna.

You have to ice them down in coolers so they go dormandt. Then before you boil them you have to spray them with water to make them conscious again. Once the water is seasoned and spiced to perfection. Just dropped them in.

OMG they are so good. My daughter Morgan and I can seriously eat our weight in them. Of Course there are Corn and polatatoes boiled with them.

We line a large picnic table with brown paper bags and pour it all out togther on the table.

It's always a great time and a great way to

eat and really be expected
to be messy.
"One of my favorite meals"
AYee!!

RANDY AND JOEY HOLDER

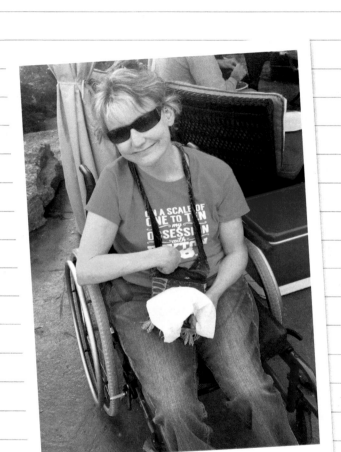

"OUR DAUGHTER, KELLEY WHITE, AT
THE CRAWFISH BOIL."

"IN THE FRONT IS MY SON-IN-LAW,
JUSTIN COOK. BEHIND HIM IS ALEX
WILLIS. KAREN KAPOSI IS ON THE LEFT."

LORRIE AND MORGAN AT McNAMARA'S IRISH PUB EVERY

ST. PADDY'S DAY FOR MUSIC AND IRISH GOOD

Now this the best and maybe one of the largest Crossants I've ever encountered.

The perfect Crossant with "Collapsible inner woven flakes" In Hale Whites words.

This is what we search for everywhere and finally found in Helsenki, Finland

"A PERFECT CROISSANT WITH COLLAPSIBLE INNER WOVEN FLAKES" - HALE WHITE

Cock-of-the-Walk

This restaraunt is on
Music Valley Drive in Nashville,
Tn.

Great Cat fish and onion rings,
and Corn bread and pickled
onions!! Oh and the fried
pickles. Shrimp too.

Relaxed country atmosphere.
One of our whole families
favorite places in Nashville
to eat. Oh I forgot great
White Beans and turnip Greens

Yum

8-1962
OFICIAL   1976

30-11

Nº 1684

MORGAN, PRESTON, AND JUSTIN COOK

"GERMAPHOBIC HALE WHITE'S SPECIAL WAY
TO HOLD THE SALT & PEPPER SHAKERS AT
RESTAURANTS TO AVOID GERMS. LOL"

Quote from Klale White
About potatoe Chips

" Due to Contamenation Concerns,
I only bite the portion of the
Chip that my fingers never
touch, Then I leave little
Crumbs in a small organized
throw away pile"
        I wish I had taken
a pic of his pile.

                    Hillarius

Recipes

Morgan Family
Hot Chicken @ Home

Although there are many Hot Chicken recipes. This one is an old family recipe that my dad, George, enjoyed making. Very different than my HotChickens.com recipe and other Nashville Hot Chicken restaurants. Still fun to eat.

Things you'll need!
Salt & pepper
All purpose unbleached flour
Can Crisco shortening
Loaf of white bread (preferably Bunny)
10 chicken breasts
2 large jars cayenne pepper or 4
1 can Hungarian paprika
5 large jars white pepper (this is what makes it hot)
wax paper
Jar of dill pickle chips

In a large electric or cast iron skillet fill halfway up with Crisco shortening and let melt on low heat. Makes about 10 pieces.

In a bowl, mix together all spices (it should make a nice orange color).

In a doubled paper grocery bag, pour in half bag of unbleached flour. Set aside.

Prepare cutting off ten 14 inch pieces of wax paper lay on pile. Set aside.

Open bread.

Clean chicken breasts.

Salt & Pepper to your liking.

Individual pieces of chicken:

Take one by one — put in spice bowl and coat well!!!

Remove and put in bag of flour. Add about 3 pieces at a time.

Turn grease up to med to high. You want grease to start your chicken as soon as chicken is dropped in.

Shake bag well with the chicken and flour together until chicken is well coated in flour.

Drop first 3 breasts in grease.

Repeat until all are cooked.

I like the electric skillet for these, it has a lid to steam the chicken for about 10 mins when its thoroughly cooked.

Note (This is not a crispy chicken recipe)

You can add spice & flour to any piece of chicken as its cooking to your taste.

2 pieces of White Bread on one piece of wax paper.

Place Chicken from skillet onto the bread then top it with the other piece of bread.

Fold wax paper to cover and steam flavors together.

Stack on top of each other on a platter.

Wait about 30 mins, unwrap, add pickles on side.

Grab some cold MILK!

ENJOY

My buddy Kenny Ortega enjoys all the pain from Hot Chicken.
I love you Kenny.

Green Chili

2 lbs ground pork
2 flat pork steaks, lots of fat
1 large strong onion
3 large cloves of garlic
About 20 small cans of Hot Diced Green Chilis
15 fresh habanero peppers
15 fresh serrano peppers
5-10 fresh ghost peppers
10 fresh jalapeno peppers
(Caution — use an electric chopper for peppers and wear rubber gloves while handling raw peppers)
3 Tbsp. black pepper
Kosher salt to taste
1 Tbsp. garlic powder
1 box chicken stock

In a large stock pot brown ground pork.

Brown cut up pork steak (leave fat on) cut into small cubes

Add large chopped onion and garlic

Brown well (if it begins to stick — pour a bit of chicken stock. Not too much as the peppers will make pretty much liquid.)

Prepare all peppers, onions, garlic etc...

After all meat is browned with onion and garlic, begin pouring in cans of green chilis. Mix in. Then add slowly all of four chopped peppers stirring well.

Add salt, pepper and garlic powder.

Again, if it looks dry pour just a bit of chicken stock.

Bring to a strong boil while folding all ingredients together.

Then cover and turn on low and simmer for less than two hours.

Longer is better.

Remember the more black pepper — the better.

Also add any other kinds of peppers you choose:

Cayenne — Red

Scorpion etc...

It up to your tongue.

GEORGE MORGAN MAKING GREEN CHILI

Quesadilla

Ingredients:
Large flour tortillas
Four cheese Mexican cheese
Canned green chilis

If you have a panini maker. Get large flour tortillas add four cheese Mexican cheese.

Large amount of green chili on top.

Put more cheese on top.

Fold where all ends are closed.

Put in Panini, close lid. Listen for sizzle. Change quesadilla's position — close.

When cheese is all melted. ENJOY.

THE MAKING OF THE BAR FOR MY NEW SPICY HOT CHICKEN RESTAURANT "THE COOP" IN PCB OPENING IN 2019

Breakfast Green Chili

Ingredients:
Flat hard tostada or soft flour or corn tortilla
Refried beans
Mexican four cheese
Canned green chili

Flat hard tostada or soft flour or corn tortilla.

Smooth on warm refried beans.

Cover with Mexican four cheese.

Cover with about 2 tbs. of warmed up green chili

Add 2 fried over medium eggs.

Add more green chili.

Top with a mound of Mexican four cheese.

All melts together.

Mmm good

Summer Fruit Salad

Ingredients:
Fresh watermelon
Fresh blueberries
Fresh lime
Fresh cilantro
Fresh serrano pepper
Fresh mint

In large clear glass bowl place out squares (small) of watermelon in bowl.

Add blueberries. Don't overwhelm with the blueberries.

Chop cilantro about a half bundle. Sprinkle in bowl

Chop serrano pepper or peppers (seeds in) to your heat level.

Squeeze whole lime into salad.

Mix gently.

Decorate at the end with fresh whole & chopped mint.

Serve chilled.

GRANDMA MORGAN
& LORRIE

Tomato Gravy

Ingredients:
2 Tbsp. bacon grease
One small white onion, cut in circles, not chopped
1 Tbsp. all purpose unbleached flour
½ cup regular tomato juice
½ cup water
½ stick real butter
Kosher salt
Black pepper

In a cast iron skillet, with about 2 Tbsp. bacon grease melted, add one small white onion. Brown onion, until good and brown. Once brown — remove from skillet and put aside or throw away (or give to Tuff, my grandson, who loves them).

Add 1 Tbsp. of all purpose unbleached flour at a time to insure you don't add too much. Flour in the grease must be firm but look spreadable.

The secret is to brown the flour dark like a rue, but do not burn (there should be non excess rolling around the skillet & it usually takes for me 2 Tbsp. of flour).

Add regular tomato juice and ½ cup water. Mix together a little tomato juice than water.

On medium heat once flour & grease are good and browned pour in water & juice stirring briskly as not to cause clumps to form in gravy. (Take your time on this process.)

Once you've stirred to a gravy consistency add 1 half stick of real butter.

Kosher salt to taste.

Lots of black pepper.

Serve on warm biscuits or toast.

Sonia's Pasta

Ingredients:
One pound regular bacon
6 raw eggs
Fettuccine
Butter
3 green onions
Black coarse pepper

Note: this dish is best served immediately — warm w/ garlic toast & beautiful white wine.

Fry one pound regular bacon to a good crispy consistency. Remove from pan. Put on a paper towel to soak up excess grease.

Boil fettuccine in large stock pot. While boiling add ½ tsp. of kosher salt. Add ½ tsp. extra virgin olive oil.

While this boils, chop up 3 green onions (green stocks included). Set aside.

Have about 6 eggs sitting ready to add.

When pasta is finished, drain (important) do not drain all the pasta's water. It is salted and has the pasta taste. Quickly put back in pan and set back on stove on low.

Quickly add the 6 raw eggs and stir in (the hot pasta will cook it).

Add stick of real butter.

Add prepared onions.

Add black coarse pepper.

Then last add your bacon crumbled by hand.

Add a sprig of basil to everyone's dish.

Serve immediately! Bon appetit!

Randy's Hard Fudge

Ingredients:
2C Sugar
3 heaping Tbsp. cocoa-chocolate
Almost full C milk
Pinch of salt
3 Tbsp. real butter
½ tsp. vanilla extract

Combine sugar, chocolate in frying pan.

Add milk.

Med high heat — bring to boil

Drop a small drip in cold water. When it reaches soft ball stage — turn heat to low.

Add butter and whip until glossy.

Stir in vanilla.

Pour in buttered flat pan.

When hardened — cut into squares.

Serve! And have milk!

Tomato Juice and Shells

Ingredients:
Kosher salt to taste
½ tsp. Worcestershire sauce
5 drops — Tabasco sauce
Black pepper to taste
½ stick of real butter
Medium size shell pasta

In a small to medium pan pour tomato juice.

Add kosher salt to taste, ½ tsp. Worcestershire sauce, 5 drops — Tabasco sauce, black pepper to taste, ½ stick of real butter

Note: You can make this as spicy as you like.

Separate pan — medium pan — boil water and add a pinch of Kosher salt.

Pour in half box of medium size shell pasta.

Boil then turn to medium heat.

Stir occasionally until shells are soft.

Strain pour back in pan. Add the other ½ stick real butter & salt to taste.

In a soup bowl pour pasta in and ladle tomato sauce on top to make soupy.

This is great with grilled cheese on a snowy date. — LM

Tuna Fish and Noodles

In a large mixing bowl empty two cans of (I prefer — Chicken of The Sea) tuna, juice and all.

Add two eggs — beaten.

Add 2 lg. cans of Cream of Mushroom soup — possible 1½ cans of the Cream of Mushroom soup.

Mix all together with salt & pepper and ½ tsp. garlic powder. Set aside.

In med pan bring water to boil add pinch of Kosher salt.

While at full boil pour in a bag of wide egg noodles.

When they are almost done, remove from heat and strain, leaving a little pasta water in bottom.

In a casserole dish (deep) coat well with Pam.

Pour pasta into premixed tuna until a nice consistency.

Pour into greased casserole dish.

Making careful holes in the mixture pour in whole milk. About halfway in mixture — Do not cover with milk.

Put lid on dish, place in 350 degree oven on bake.

Bake for one hour or until its all bubbling.

The last 10 min you can take the lid off to make the top crunchy or add cheese.

This is great with LeSueur Green Peas.

That's how Randy likes it.

Aunt Kate's Gom Cookies

Ingredients:
1 C shortening and 1 C sugar, creamed together
2 eggs beaten
4 tsp. baking powder
4 C all purpose unbleached flour
1 C milk – whole

(We use a biscuit cutter to cut the cookies)

Mix all ingredients together.

Roll out – cut cookies

Bake at 450 degrees – 7-8 min and watch closely as not to burn

Thank you Aunt Kate!

MORGAN & PARKER
LYNN COOK

Wendy's Taco Soup

As I'm always dieting off and on, this is a soup my niece Wendy introduced me to.

Very high fiber and full of protein

Ingredients:

2 cans white hominy

1 can black beans

1 can pinto beans

1 can "red" kidney beans

2 cans rotel — hot or not

1 can chicken stock

1 pkg. taco seasoning (low sodium)

1 pkg. Ranch dressing mix

The soup is easy to make and ready in no time.

My favorite:
Mom's Beef Stroganoff

Serves about 6

Brown cubed sirloin steak and cut up onion together, cook on side bag of egg noodles — set aside fresh sautéed mushrooms cook.

When steak, onion and mushrooms are done pour mushrooms in pan with the meat & onions.

Note: don't skimp on the shrooms.

Add 2 cans of Cream of Mushroom soup

$\frac{3}{4}$ C sour cream

Salt & pepper to taste

Add 1 tsp. of garlic powder

When all is cooking well with each other add $\frac{1}{2}$ stick of butter.

Add good unsweet red wine, not much — just enough to taste its flavoring. Probably a good year of Cab or Sauvignon.

Add cooked noodles to stroganoff.

Stir and cook on low until ready to serve.

Mom's Scalded Corn Cakes

These are great with a pot of beans & onions.

Ingredients:
1½ C corn meal
2 C water
1 tsp. salt

Boil water and gradually add corn meal & salt.

Pour in a small amount of cold water just to start its process of cooling down.

Set in refrigerator for 20 min or so until there is no gooey or sticky consistency to touch.

Fold into flat ball patties (small size of smashed golf balls).

Fry in hot grease and fry quickly — about 5 min.

Take out slice, put real butter in between top & bottom.

They are also great with honey or syrup.

WITH MY MOM,
MOTHER'S DAY, 2018

Granny Faye Whitley's Chocolate Gravy

Ingredients:

2 C milk

½ C sugar

3 Tbsp. all purpose flour

1 Tbsp. cocoa

Over medium heat, combine already mixed flour, cocoa & sugar.

Add milk and stir together until thick.

She cooked this for Keith every time we went home to Sandy Hook.

Very crunchy bacon with his mom's chocolate gravy.

PRESTON COOK,
TUFF WHITLEY
& LORRIE

Grandma Morgan's Pankaus

Okay, this one is difficult. This is a German dish that my dad found from my Grandma Morgan. "Like sausage." Time consuming. Requires a meat grinder.

Ingredients:

¾ lbs. pork liver

¾ lbs. pork shoulder

Barely cover with water in a pan and simmer on low. Cook until liver is tender. Maybe two hours. Take meat out of broth and grind in large bowl. Put back in broth. Be sure it not too watery. On the side, in another bowl – 3 C plain corn meal, 1 tsp. salt.

Pour boiling water over meal until wet, add cold water to the consistency of a hoe cake – medium firm – no lumps.

Bring broth to boil – add corn meal mixture gradually stirring constantly. This is tricky.

When it starts to get dry looking – it will pop up at you in bubbles – keep stirring (wooden spoon) takes about 15 min for this to cook. When it gets thick pour into loaf pans. (spray a little with Pam first). Let it cool over night or all day.

Slice into ½ inch slices and coat each slice in all purpose flour and fry in hot grease.

Great as a breakfast meat.

Also if you like, try syrup on top.

Kristi's Slaw Salad

Serves quite a bit.

Ingredients:
½ head cabbage – cut up
3 cucumbers
2 fresh jalapeno peppers
1 fresh habanero pepper (optional)
½ jar pickled banana peppers (pour out juice and chop)
4 green onions
Fresh cilantro
Small grape tomatoes
½ - 1 Tbsp. of cumin
Garlic powder & salt & pepper to taste
2-3 tsp. of celery seed – important
Hellman's Mayo – not too much – approx. 2-3 tablespoons

Chop cabbage, long ways then in half.

Chop all together.

Add mayo last and serve.

Tumi (Fumi?) Salad

Ingredients:

1 ½ bags slaw
8 green onions
8 Tbsp. sesame seeds — brown
8 Tbsp. slivered almonds — I like to brown them
2 pkg. ramen noodles, crushed

Dressing:
4 Tbsp. sugar
1 tsp. black pepper
4 Tbsp. rice vinegar
2 tsp. salt
½ - 1 C oil

Mix cabbage & onions at last minute, add almonds & seed and crushed noodles. Pour dressing over mix just before serving.

JESSE KEITH
WHITLEY

Aunt Jean's
Cracker Jack

Ingredients:
1 C Brer Rabbit Molasses
1 C white karo
2 C sugar
½ C water
1 tsp. baking soda

Cook all together — wooden spoon. Pull spoon out of mixture if it looks like a whispy thread — remove and add to white popped corn.

Careful mixing with your hands. It can burn and stick to your fingers. I always mix in large brown wooden bowl.

LORRIE & MORGAN

Mom's Christmas Cookies

Ingredients:
Cream together ¾ C shortening, part butter
1 C sugar
2 eggs
1 tsp. Vanilla
Then add flour mixture
2 ½ C all purpose flour
1 tsp. baking powder
1 tsp. salt

Mix with wooden spoon in bowl — chill for 1 hr.

Roll thin bake at 400 degrees for 6-8 min.

Icing:
½ box of powdered sugar
2 Tbsp. melted butter
1 tsp. vanilla
Add whole milk until spreadable

Add in separate cups food coloring if desired.

Merry Christmas.

Mom's Vegetable Soup
revised by Lorrie

Ingredients:
1 piece Sirloin Steak (I prefer a lot of marble for flavoring), cut into cubes
2 cloves of garlic – sliced thin
1 lg. onion
2 bay leaves
4 stalks celery

Brown beef & onions & garlic together. Careful not to brown garlic. (Have some beef stock on hand and tomato juice).
Once meat is brown (add your choice of veggies)
2 cans Shoe Peg corn
1 can LeSueur peas
1 can green beans
Pkg. of fresh cut crinkle carrots or cut your own
1 can lima beans
Add half bottle of tomato juice
Mix in a little water or beef stock (I prefer beef stock)
Add one handful white rice.
And one handful elbow macaroni.
2-3 Drops of Louisiana hot sauce
Kosher salt to taste
Lots of black pepper
Small amount of garlic powder
A pinch of Italian seasoning

If desired, at the very last you can add sliced frozen okra (not too much). Cook well. Again, add what veggies you prefer. Add stock & juice to make more soupy.

My Chili (Red)

Ingredients:
1 ½ lb ground chuck
1 lg. yellow onion
2 cans pinto beans
Tomato juice and a good Mexican beer
1 ½ lb ground chuck
1 lg. yellow onion
1 Tbsp. apple cider vinegar
Almost one jar of chili powder
Salt & pepper to taste.

Brown together ground chuck and yellow onion. Pour in 2 can pinto beans (I like Lucy's with pork in it). Add part tomato juice and a good Mexican beer (part beer), 1 Tbsp. apple cider vinegar, almost one jar of chili powder. You want your chili dark red. Salt & pepper to taste.

That's all.

I like to add a part of my Ohio heritage to chili sometimes.

Cooked pasta (spaghetti) add to bowl first then pour in chili.

Go Bucks.

Fondue Barbecue Sauce

Ingredients:
½ C water
¼ C vinegar
1 Tbsp. mustard
1/3 C brown sugar
Paprika to taste probably
¾ Tbsp. Tabasco
2 Tbsp. lemon juice
1 finely ground onion

Boil, let simmer for at least 45 min to thicken. Serve room temp.

MA MORGAN'S
86TH BIRTHDAY

Ron's Chancey's New Brunswick Stew

Ingredients:
Nice size hen
Chopped tomatoes
2 lg. lemons
2 cans peeled tomatoes
1 can crushed tomatoes
1 medium size chopped onion
5 or 6 stalks celery — chopped
2 pkgs frozen okra
3 cans shoe peg corn
5 Tbsp. Worcestershire sauce
Lawry's season salt
Lots of black pepper!!
1½ stick real butter

Boil in large stock pan nice size hen. Put all in stock put. The longer it cooks the better it is. Add some tomato juice if desired — not too much.

Zucchini Bread Ma's

Ingredients:
3 eggs – separate white from yolks
1 C oil
2 C sugar
2 C grated zucchini
3 tsp. vanilla
3 C all purpose unbleached flour
1 tsp. baking soda
1 tsp. cinnamon
1 tsp. salt

Grease 2 loaf pans then flour them. Combine beaten egg yolks, oil, sugar & vanilla – beat together. Mix dry ingredients together – flour, sugar, salt & soda. Then add zucchini. Mix well. Beat egg whites, let peak fold egg whites into batter. Bake at 325 degrees about 1 hr.

Dad's Superman Egg

Ingredients:
Bread
Egg
Salt to taste
Pepper to taste
Oil

Use little grease in skillet, very little. Put a whole in one white or wheat piece of bread — size of a donut hole let grease get hot. Place bread in hot skillet on med to low then crack egg and pour in the hole of bread. Cook then flip to desired consistency. Flip each over and serve with breakfast meats etc... Salt & pepper to taste.

RANDY'S BIRTHDAY

COWBOY STEAK

Mom's Salmon Patties

One of my favorites with mac & cheese or shells & red sauce.

1 Can pink salmon (do not drain)

In a mixing bowl smash with fork 1 egg beaten — place aside
approx. 1 or 1½ sleeves of Ritz Crackers (crushed)
¼ C corn meal.

Add egg, salt, pepper, garlic powder to taste.

You can add chopped onion or fresh jalapenos if desired. Pat out
in small to medium patties and fry in hot grease until golden
brown.

PRESTON LOVES CHOCOLATE

Fried Corn

Ingredients:
6 Lg ears of corn (I prefer white)
2 Tbsp. bacon grease
½ Stick real butter
Flour
Salt to taste
Pepper to taste

With a sharp knife cut off the cobb, then scrape until nothing, including juices, are left on the cob. (Try to keep down in the sink in your bowl to avoid splatter everywhere).

Use a cast iron skillet. 2 Tbsp. bacon grease ½ stick real butter. Put corn in and cook medium until thickened. If you want thicker add small amount of all purpose flour. Let cook. Add salt and pepper to taste. Serve hot.

Steamed Artichoke

This is great for out at the pool, boat, or just shared with friends.

Ingredients:
Artichoke
1 lemon
1 stick real butter
Kosher salt

In a large steamer pan place already to go artichoke.

1 Lg. Artichoke — trim off all pointed stickers on the ends of each leaf. Cut off bottom large stem so the choke sits flat. On the side, melt one stick of real butter — squeeze one whole juicy lemon watch for dropping seeds!! Pinch of kosher salt. I put it in a small pan on stove just enough to melt. Put lemon in after you remove from heat. Steam artichoke for at least 45 min or until its leaves are tender. Remove from steam, set in shallow med sized bowl. With two forks gently pull down the leaves to open (the tender parts are toward the middle). Remove prickles from body of stem. After the choke is open gently pour butter, lemon & salt mix all over. Be sure to well saturate.

This is a finger food. When room temp serve before butter gets hard in bowl. Pull off leaf at a time and with your teeth scrape off the meaty part of leaves.

So Good.

The middle is the gold!

I made this all summer, great with a non-sweet white wine.

Lorrie's Clams and Linguine

Ingredients:
1 stick real butter melted brown
2 small shallots – sliced
2 garlic cloves – chopped
About 1-2 lbs of clams
Add 1 bay leaf
Kosher salt to taste
Black pepper to taste
Crab boil (Old Bay) to taste
Fresh basil

In a medium skillet, brown ½ stick butter, shallots, garlic on med heat. Add ½ bottle of unsweet white wine. Put in other ½ stick of butter.

On the side bring your water for linguine to boil. Add a pinch of salt when water boils. Add linguine to full boil. Stir often so pasta does not stick together.

*When your broth has settled to a med boil add rinsed clams. Be sure all are closed tightly (if some are a little open – discard them.)

If clams all are open except a few remove unopened ones and discard. Drain well done pasta. Save some of the pasta juice in bottom of pan. This gives a richer pasta taste to the dish (not too much)

In large but not deep bowl place pasta and pour clams & broth on top. Mix well. Garnish with sprigs of fresh basil.

Great with a Riesling wine.

Randy's favorite.

Thai Coconut Soup

Prep time 10 min

Ingredients:
4 C Chicken stock
1 (15) ounce can coconut milk
1 Tbsp. fish sauce
1 2 inch piece fresh ginger — peeled and sliced
1-2 serrano peppers — sliced
1 stalk lemon grass — cut into 1 inch pieces
2 Tbsp. fresh lime juice
½ lb peeled and deveined shrimp
½ 8 ounce package baby bella mushrooms
2 Tbsp. fresh cilantro leaves

Combine first 6 ingredients in large sauce pan over medium heat. Bring to boil; reduce heat and simmer 10 minutes. Stir in lime juice. Add shrimp, and simmer 10 more minutes. Discard ginger and lemon grass. Stir in sliced mushrooms and cilantro.

Makes 7 C.

I like to sprinkle in crushed red peppers. Lots.

Marinara Sauce
by Lorrie

This is what I cooked for Randy the first time I made him dinner at his house.

Ingredients:
1 box tomato sauce
½ stick real butter
3 garlic cloves
2 bay leaves
1 block Parmesan cheese
Fresh basil
Olive oil
Coconut oil
2 shallots
Fresh oregano
Fresh thyme
Red wine – cab

In a large sauce pan or deep skillet melt 1 tsp. coconut oil. Combine sliced shallots and sliced garlic (do not let garlic get brown). When shallots & garlic are clear put in ½ stick butter. Pour in tomato sauce. Add bay leaves, chopped oregano, chopped thyme – about half C of each. Kosher salt to taste. Black pepper. Add about ½ cup red cabernet dry wine. Add other half stick of butter. Slice Parmesan cheese on the side. Cook about 1 hr on low stirring occasionally. Cook your favorite pasta and pour your sauce onto pasta in a bowl. Garnish with fresh basil on top and Parmesan cheese. I prefer a great cab with this meal followed by a chilled sm glass of Limoncello.

Mom's Dressing
revised by Lorrie

Turkey time.

This recipe depends on how many people you are serving.

Ingredients:
2 bags Pepperidge Farm Cornbread Stuffing mix
Half stalk celery
2 boxes low sodium chicken stock
1 whole loaf white bread
Optional — 1-2 cans fresh oysters from butcher or seafood department (not from shelves)
2 Tbsp. sage
2 eggs (beaten first)
1 Lrg onion
Salt to taste
Pepper to taste

Start by cleaning out your turkey. Put cleaned turkey aside — remove all giblets from inside the turkey. Empty into lg. sauce pan and bring to boil w/ water (make full) Cook at least 1 hour or longer if you can. Set aside.

In large sauce pan of water cook celery and onion together. Boil — simmer — turn off and put aside pan!!! In a large crock pot combine all ingredients. Add ½ broth from giblets and cut the liver up and add it as well. Add chicken stock to desired thickness. You may have to add more along the way. To do so dig a hole in dressing and pour in hole as not to make the dressing mushy. Salt & Pepper. I like lots of pepper & sage. (This is just guidelines) ("These"....not "this")

If desired you can put some dressing with added oysters (juice included) and stuff in your turkey — tie his legs together with cooking string. Use a lg. browning bag and follow directions on the box of bags. Very important. Happy Thanksgiving.

GRANDMA GOM'S TEAPOT.

LOTTIE LOVES TEA

Krisi's Collard and Turnip Greens

Ingredients:
¾ pound sliced bacon
3 C Sliced onion
8 cloves minced garlic
3 Tbsp. salt
¾ cayenne pepper
1 quart water
1 C or 12-ounce beer
¼ C white distilled vinegar
2 Tbsp. molasses
5 lbs greens / half collard / half turnip or mustard greens

In a large pot cook bacon until it has rendered most of its fat about 5-6 min. Add garlic & onions, salt, cayenne, black pepper and cook all until wilted about 4 min – onions, etc...

Add water, beer, vinegar, molasses, bring to a boil. Begin adding greens in batches pressing down with wooden spoon to submerge in hot liquid, adding more as they will. When all greens are added – reduce heat to a simmer. Stir occasionally with the lid on for about 1- ½ hours or until tender. Note: be sure greens are cleaned and hard stems are removed.

My Southern Chicken Salad

Ingredients:
2 bone-in chicken thighs
1 chicken breast bone-in
2-3 stalks of celery
3 green onions
C of red grapes — no seeds
Slivered or whole almonds
1 ½ large Tbsp. Hellman's Mayo
1 Tbsp. Dijon mustard
1 Tbsp. 7-Up
Kosher salt to taste
Pepper to taste
Paprika to taste

Boil in sauce pan until they are tender and falling off the bone. Cut up 2-3 stalks of celery. Slivered or whole almonds (I like to brown mine — makes a beautiful taste. If fall brown — turn over on broil and watch closely as not to brown. Place done tender chicken on cutting board and cut into chunks. In nice size mixing bowl mix chicken, chopped celery, chopped green onion, chopped grapes. (Add cilantro if desired) I prefer not. Add about 1 ½ lrg Tbsp. Hellman's Mayo, 1 Tbsp. Dijon mustard, 1 Tbsp. 7-Up. Salt — kosher, pepper, paprika to taste. Add almonds at last and fold in. I like to put in a nice wheat pita bread.

Healthy Cado Anytime

Ingredients:

1 avocado / sliced in half — de-seed

~~Boil 2~~ eggs — soft

Steam a few asparagus stems

½ C cilantro

1 serrano pepper chopped or sliced.

Peel eggs, slice. Cut asparagus into small bites. Place eggs on top of avocado. Place asparagus on top sides of avocado.

Note: I like to put peppers in the hole of the avocado before place eggs on top. Little salt — coarse, pepper garnish with fresh basil. The great thing about this dish is you can add whatever you like to Cado. Small boiled shrimp & lime juice & cilantro — or cooked small cherry tomatoes. Water cress & pecans etc...etc... I love this in the summer.

LORRIE MAKING
CHICKEN AND
DUMPLINGS

Another Great Summer or Picnic Finger Food

Ingredients:
1 dozen eggs
Tbsp. Hellman's Mayo
1 Tbsp. vinegar — apple cider
1½ Tbsp. regular yellow mustard
Kosher coarse salt
4 avocados
Chives
Paprika to taste

Boil 1 dozen eggs. Cut in half — remove egg yolks and put in a mixing bowl. Smash with fork. Add Tbsp. Hellman's Mayo. 1 Tbsp. vinegar — apple cider 1 ½ Tbsp. regular yellow mustard. Mix well — add back in egg holes. On the side, cut into small squares 4 avocados or desired amount. Squeeze 1 whole lime over them in bowl, add kosher salt & chopped chives. Place on top of deviled eggs. Add paprika & coarse salt.

Lorrie's Guacamole Salad

Serves 4

Ingredients:
4 good sized avos de-seeded
1 large tomato
3-4 green onions or red onions
1 hot habanero pepper
2 serrano peppers
1 jalapeno pepper
1 lime
1 Tbsp. olive oil
2 Tbsp. garlic powder
Paprika

Using a spoon, scrape out of outer shell into mixing bowl.
Using chopper, chop 1 large tomato (not too fine) combine with
avo on cutting board. Chop 3 or 4 green onions or red onion (if
preferred) use all green onions, 1 hot habanero pepper chopped,
2 serrano peppers, 1 jalapeno pepper. Squeeze 1 lime into bowl.
Add 1 Tbsp. olive oil. Add 2 Tbsp. garlic powder. Kosher salt,
pepper. When mixed together add paprika on top. Olé.

Broccoli Salad

Ingredients:

1/3 Cup champagne vinegar

¼ Cup olive oil

1 fresh serrano chili pepper – thinly sliced

½ Lb. broccoli

¼ C drained and dried mandarin oranges

½ C dry roasted cashews (again I like to brown my cashews)

RANDY WHITE

Shrimp in a Basket
(aluminum basket)

This is a new recipe for me. I kind of made this one up this summer. But its great and light.

Ingredients:
Heavy duty aluminum foil (2 pieces cut in about 16' long)
2 Lbs. of fresh (peel on) Tiger Shrimp
1 ½ lime — squeeze on shrimp
Sea salt
Old Bay Seasoning
2 green onions — cut up
¾ stick of real butter
Louisiana Hot Sauce
1 whole lemon
1 bay leaf
1 avocado
½ bunch fresh cilantro
Paprika
Tortillas

Place shrimp in a strainer — set aside until its pretty dry. Place on double sheets of foil. Fold sides up so nothing runs out. 1 ½ lime — squeeze on shrimp, couple pinches of sea salt, Old Bay Seasoning — load it up! Sprinkle green onions on shrimp, ¾ stick real butter, add a few drops of Louisiana Hot sauce. Cut lemon in small slices and leave in while cooking. 1 bay leaf. Close foil where nothing will leak out but make the top loose so it can also steam inside. Place on grill for 25-30 min on low heat-med.

On the side cut 1 whole avocado into pieces. Half bunch of fresh cilantro. Chop rough. Set aside. When done — shrimp will be nice and orange & white. (careful of steam when opening foil) Place in clean serving bowl. Add ¼ stick of butter. Sprinkle with paprika. Top with avocado & cilantro. Serve alone or with tortillas. Whew!

Mom's Fried Corn

Ingredients:
Six large ears of corn (I prefer white)
2 Tbsp. bacon grease
½ Stick real butter
Flour
Salt to taste
Pepper to taste

Cut off cobb & scrape off cobb to get all the juices. Use cast iron skillet, 2 Tbsp. bacon grease in skillet and ½ stick real butter. On med heat — add corn and let it thicken (optional) if you like it thicker, Randy says add 1 Tbsp. all purpose flour. Salt & pepper to taste. I like to add a lot of butter.

Morgan Family Milk Gravy

Ingredients:
2 Tbsp. bacon grease
All purpose flour
Whole milk
Salt
Black pepper

2 Tbsp. bacon grease. Add all purpose flour to grease in cast iron skillet. Flour should be a nice consistency and turn to a darkish brown – much like roux (the flour is a guessing game). Start with one Tbsp. then if you need more add a little at a time. You don't want it clumpy. Keep on med to high heat. Pour in whole milk stirring constantly – stir until thickened. Turn down heat. Add salt & lots of black pepper. Add ½ stick real butter.

Mom's Sloppy Joe's

Ingredients:
2 lbs ground chuck
1 green bell pepper
1 onion – chopped fine
2 jars Heinz Chili Sauce
Clove
Salt
Pepper
Garlic powder

Cook & brown together 2 jars Heinz Chili Sauce. Add to meat after it browns well. Add salt & pepper & garlic powder to taste. Add ground clove. Taste after it all cooks together to see if it has enough clove. This is the secret to her great Sloppy Joes. Not too much clove and not too little. Cook until most juice is gone. Put on bun and have fun.

Jesse's Warm Potato Salad

Ingredients:
1 bag red potatoes — peeled and chopped into squares
1 dozen eggs
Regular jar Duke's Mayonnaise
Tony Chachere's Louisiana Seasoning
Paprika

Boil eggs with potatoes. Using large spoon remove eggs from boiled water. Making sure potatoes are done not squishy. Peel eggs. Drain potatoes. Chop eggs bluntly (big chops). Put back finished warm potatoes in pot. Add almost whole jar of Dukes Mayo. Mash & mix to consistency you desire. Add Tony's seasoning to taste. Serve warm. Sprinkle paprika on top to serve.

Marty's Daddy
Sausage by George

"This old family tradition doesn't have much in the way of measurements. It's one of those recipes you just kind of got to eyeball it." Mmm.

Marty learned it from watching Dad make it when we were all little. Marty was responsible for the "hand making" once Dad had all the ingredients in place.

Warning: mixing real cold pork will make your knuckle joints hurt...

Only ground pork. No added parts, usually found in commercial sausage. So the taste and texture is so enjoyably good.

Ingredients:
2 Lbs ground pork
Ground sage
Crushed red pepper
Salt
White pepper
Habanero pepper

2 lbs. ground pork in mixing bowl. Add a "generous" portion of ground sage. Sage to taste! Add nice medium layer of coarse ground black pepper, until sage is covered right. Cover with a layer of crushed red pepper. Depending on how much hot you like it — use your own judgment, we like it hot. Lightly dust with salt

— to taste. Add a tsp. white pepper, more or less to your taste.
1 tsp. cayenne pepper. (If desired with caution add a touch of
ground Habanero) optional.

Mix all together with your hands, kneading well until fully
blended — no pockets of spice visible. Pat into a big ole ball...
then pinch out enough to make a patty that is about $\frac{1}{2}$ inch to
$\frac{3}{4}$ inch thick by about 3 inches wide... (it going to shrink).

Fry on medium high heat in a skillet until brown and slightly
crisp on the sides...Slap it on a piece of fresh white bread or
warm biscuit or fry up some eggs with buttered toast and have
a nice cold glass of milk handy...That's the way we do it in the
Morgan family for the last 50 years or so.

Mussels in White Wine Sauce

Ingredients:
1 stick real butter
1 shallot
2 Or 3 cloves garlic
½ bottle non-sweet white wine
Mussels
Kosher salt
Coarse pepper
1 lemon
Italian parsley
Italian bread

In skillet melt on stick real butter. Chop one whole shallot and slice 2 or 3 cloves of garlic. Saute until shallots and garlic are clear. Slowly pour in a non-sweet white wine, about ½ bottle. When heated, add Kosher Salt & coarse pepper. Add mussels and close lid. On the side in measuring cup melt one stick real butter and juice one whole lemon. Heat in microwave or on stove. Mussels cook until all are open — about 20 min — (discard any unopened mussels) Pour mussels and all in a nice pretty bowl. Lastly, pour over all the heated lemon & butter. Dress with fresh Italian parsley. Serve it up with a great loaf of Italian bread to sop up the juice. Serve with cold white wine. :)

Mom's Artichoke Dip

2 cans artichokes – chopped fine
2/3 C Parmesan cheese
1 C mayo
Mix all together.
¼ C sour cream
1/8 tsp. Tabasco – optional

Mix all well.

Put in sprayed Pyrex. Put in oven. Bake 350 degrees for 30 min.

Great for parties.

Possum's Pineapple Casserole

1 Lrg. can pineapple chunks — drained.

1 ½ C grated cheddar cheese

¾ C sugar

3 Tbsp. all purpose flour

Mix flour & sugar with juice drained off pineapple.

1 melted stick real butter

1 sleeve of Ritz Crackers crushed

Paused by Mom.

Forgot what she did with rest of recipe. LMAO.

Good luck.

Randy's Egg Gravy

Ingredients:
1 stick real butter
1 ½ - 2 Tbsp. all purpose flour
6-9 boiled, peeled chopped eggs
Salt to taste
Pepper to taste

1 Stick real butter. Melt in iron skillet. 1 ½ - 2 Tbsp. of all purpose flour and brown in butter to a good consistency for gravy. Nice & thick. Salt & Pepper to taste. 1 pinch of sugar. Add 6-9 Boiled peeled and chopped eggs. Stir in! Return to a medium boil and serve hot over toast preferably (better on toast) or biscuit.

Randy's Homemade Pineapple Sherbet

Ingredients:
1 Can crushed pineapple
1 Can Eagle Brand milk
1 ~~2~~ liter bottle of Orange Crush

Pour all into cylinder of ice cream freezer. Close lid – plug in.
Add layer of ice. Add layer of rock salt. Repeat layers 3 or 4
times or as needed. Newer machines take less time. This recipe is
real! In a 5 quart ice cream freezer.

Randy's Famous Banana Bread

"Trademarked"

In large mixing bowl:
2 C all purpose flour
1 ½ Tbsp. baking powder
½ Tbsp. baking soda
¼ Tbsp. salt
1/8 T cinnamon
Mix together.

In another bowl:
5 over-ripened bananas (do not use hard bananas)
1 C sugar
1 C veg oil
2 eggs, beaten
Smash all together with a potato smasher or large fork. Pour in mixed ingredients all together. Mix well.

½ C pecans, chopped
½ C walnuts, chopped
Leave a few whole for topping when bread is done. Some chopped as well.

Best way that Randy prepares so bread is nice and fluffy is to divide mixture first into a muffin pan well-greased ½ full. Then in one loaf pan well-greased pour remainder mixture. Once poured, garnish of all bread with the nuts put aside.
Bake at 350 degrees for 55 min. Remove muffins after 20 min.
Place in center of oven. Let cool then remove and slice.

Happy Fall.

Hot !!!
Fresh Garden Salsa

Fresh tomatoes about 6 or 7 or more (peeled)
1 Lrg. yellow onion — chopped fine
6 jalapenos — chopped
6 habaneros — chopped
6 serranos — chopped
Half bunch of cleaned cilantro — chop rough

Add kosher salt & pepper & garlic powder. 1 lime squeezed all on ingredients. Stir & serve with chips.

Randy's Paper Bag Ham

Pick out a good, fatty whole bone-in ham. Preheat oven to 260 degrees. Turn the ham fatty side up and and make a 1/2 inch deep "checkerboard" cut across the top.

In a small bowl, mix brown sugar and honey together (amount all depend on the size of the ham and the size of your sweet tooth) and microwave until liquefied. Brush the liquid honey mixture on the checkerboard cut, fatty side of the ham.

Slide the ham into a brown paper bag and fold edges shut. Lace folded edges with toothpicks to keep it closed. Place the ham into a roasting pan with a rack.

Put in the oven at 260 degrees until the ham is fully cooked (use your meat thermometer to ensure the ham reaches the proper temperature (internal temp of 140 degrees F, oven time may range from 2 – 3 hours). Remove from the oven and tear open the bag to reveal a beautiful brown honey baked ham. Let stand before serving.

Hi everyone, please keep in mind that my journal entries were made on bumpy highways and back roads across the USA and beyond .... Please excuse the scribbles, typos, grammatical errors and/or food and wine stains!

:-)

Disclaimer

Some of the measurements in these recipes may not be quite accurate! Due to drinking wine and cooking. I love to cook and drink my wine and listen to all different types of music so Some of the exact measurments may be a tad off. As my mom would say, "Use your own judgement"

Period of previous stay ....30. days

[handwritten signature]

My special Thanks to:

My family, for always loving me unconditionally.

My children, Morgan & Justin Cook, Jesse Whitley,
and my grandchildren for being my everything.

My husband Randy, who loves to experience new cuisine as
much as I do, and for always being willing to try some stage
dish and mostly for loving me.

All my loyal fans, for allowing me to do what I love to do.

My manager and management team for reading this book
over over again, lol.

My assistant Sheila for taking care of me on the road
and anywhere I go.

My good boy band and road manager for making the road
so much fun and prayerful.

My dogs Weezy and Puddin' for eating the scraps
I didn't want.

- Lorrie Morgan